·CHESHIRE·

Frontispiece: Cholmondeley Castle

·CHESHIRE·

PHOTOGRAPHS BY
GEOFF MORGAN

·LEGEND BOOKS·

First published in Great Britain by
LEGEND BOOKS,
55 London Road, Alderley Edge,
Cheshire SK9 7DY.

© Legend Books 1987
ISBN 0 9512661 0 1

Photographs: Geoff Morgan
Design and layout: Margaret Morgan BA
Typeset in 11/13pt Monophoto Baskerville
Printed by Jolly & Barber Ltd, Rugby

Acknowledgements:
Our grateful thanks for their assistance to
Mr & Mrs Barnett at Overton Hall Farm,
Mr David Plastow and Mr Michael Weatherby of
Rolls Royce Motors Ltd.

Every care is taken with the information presented
in this book. Neither the author nor the publisher
can accept responsibility for consequences of
errors or omissions.

Front cover: Little Moreton Hall
Back cover: Alderley Edge
Endpapers: Half-timbered buildings, Nantwich

INTRODUCTION

Cheshire is a varied county, bounded by the
Derbyshire hills in the east, the Wirral in the west;
Manchester in the north and Audlem in the south.
A county of plains and water, hills and fine houses;
the old monuments of our industrial past and the
technology of the present, all set amidst the enduring
agriculture of this historically interesting and pic-
turesque county.

No one book can capture all this, but what we
have portrayed is the visual essence. For those
who know the county it will remind them of its
treasures, for those who do not it will inspire to
discover. For all, we hope it will present
surprises . . . .

MAP OF CHESHIRE, showing places
mentioned in this book.

Map taken from original 1:300 000 series,
Copyright © John Bartholomew & Son Limited MCMLXXXVII.
Reproduced with permission.

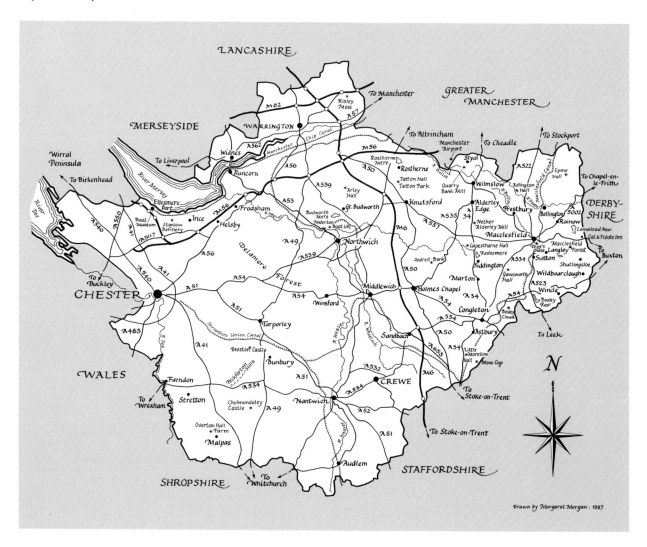

Drawn by Margaret Morgan : 1987

INDEX

* not open to the public
† party visits only, by arrangement

Opposite: Astbury. The parish church of St. Mary has two towers. The one linked to the north aisle dates from the Norman period, the tall spire was added 300 years later. The second was built onto the west end of the church in the fifteenth century.

Previous pages, left: Alderley Edge.

Right: Alderley Edge. Entrance to the old copper workings. The Edge is a wooded sandstone escarpment, with superb views over the surrounding countryside. There are tales of a Wizard and sleeping warriors, reputed to be the Knights of King Arthur, which add to its atmosphere of mystery.

Above: Artist's Lane, Alderley Edge.

Opposite: The Anderton Boat Lift. Built in 1875 to connect the Trent & Mersey Canal with the River Weaver, 50ft below. It was closed to traffic in 1982, but is now undergoing restoration.

Opposite: Arley Hall. The home of the Egerton-Warburton family for over 500 years, the present house was built in the early Victorian period, in the Jacobean style.

Below: Adlington Hall, owned by the Legh family since 1315. The house is partly half-timbered, with 18th century additions in the neo-classical style built of Cheshire brick.

Opposite: Bunbury Mill. A 17th century water mill originally for grinding corn from the Peckforton estate.

Below: Bosley Cloud and reservoir.

Below and opposite: Bramhall Hall. A fine 15th century half-timbered house owned by the Davenport family until 1877.

Building styles typical of Cheshire

Above left: Half-timbered and thatched, from the south-west of the county close to its borders with Wales and Shropshire.

Below left: Brick with slate roof. Central Cheshire, but can be seen throughout the county. The bricks are not consistent in colour, due to uneven firing.

Below: Built onto and out of large blocks of red Bunter sandstone. Here the house has been white-washed, probably to unify the stone with a later brick extension. Seen in the north-west of the county around Chester.

Below: Cheshire landscape. A patchwork of rich farmland near Malpas.

Opposite: Beeston Castle. Built as part of the Welsh border defences, this 11th century castle on its rugged cliff can be seen for miles across the Cheshire plain.

CHESTER: the county town

The old bridge across the River Dee.

Below and right: Chester cathedral. The ring of 10
bells no longer hangs in the central sandstone
tower, but in a separate campanile nearby.

King Charles' Tower. From this high viewpoint on the city walls, Charles I watched his defeated army return after the Battle of Rowton Moor.

Roman Gardens. A collection of pillars and other
stonework from Roman times, brought from
various sites in the city.

Below and right: The Rows. Shops on two levels in heavily decorated half-timbered style. Although origins are based in the mediaeval period, much of it was built or restored in the Victorian era.

The Queen's Park foot bridge across the River
Dee.

The Groves.

Below: Part of the Roman Walls.

Opposite: The magnificent clock on Eastgate.

ANTIQVI COLANT ANTIQVVM DIERVM
B C ROBERTS MAYOR 1897
J G HOLMES MAYOR 1898

Below: Crewe station, the well-known railway junction. The Crewe Arms hotel is in the background.

Right: 'Hardwicke', a locomotive built for the London & North Western Railway in 1873 at Crewe Works.

Below: Moorland near the Cat & Fiddle, the highest inn in Cheshire (1600ft above sea level).

Opposite, top left: The famous inn sign.

Top right: Steeplejack Fred Dibnah's steam-driven road roller outside the inn.

Below: Heavy winter snows sometimes make the A537 from Macclesfield to Buxton impassable.

Cholmondeley Castle, near Malpas. The gardens
are open to the public, but the castle is not.

Capesthorne Hall. The home of the Bromley-Davenports, a family connected with this part of Cheshire since the Norman conquest.

Left: The felon's head with a rope around the neck is part of the Davenport coat of arms.

Below: The lake.

Over page, left: The canals that criss-cross the countryside were once used for freight transport, but now provide pleasure for many.

Right: Delamere Forest, the remnants of the ancient mixed woodland which covered about 12000 acres in the time of the Ancient Britons.

Opposite: Dunham Massey, near Altrincham. Once the home of Lady Jane Grey. (National Trust).

Below: The Orangery.

ELLESMERE PORT:
The Boat Museum.

Below: The 'border' bridge across the River Dee at Farndon. The opposite bank is Wales.

Opposite: Forest Chapel, in Macclesfield Forest. The Rushbearing Ceremony takes place every August.

Frodsham, looking north towards Runcorn and
the River Mersey.

Helsby Hill, from Frodsham.

Gawsworth Hall. The present half-timbered house was built in the late 15th century by the Fittons. Mary Fitton was reputedly Shakespeare's 'Dark Lady' of the sonnets.

Great Budworth, a close little village of brick and timber houses.

Below and following page: Jodrell Bank radio telescope. The 250ft white dish can be seen from many parts of Cheshire. It was completed in 1957 for the University of Manchester.

Ince Marshes, with part of the power station
complex in the background.

Above: ICI. Imperial Chemical Industries have several large establishments in the county. The picture shows part of Mond Division at Northwich.

Opposite: Jenkin Chapel, Saltersford. The chapel stands at the junction of three former salt routes or salters ways.

Below and opposite: Knutsford. The Ruskin Rooms were designed by a late 19th century adventurer, Richard Harding Watt. Built in the 18th century Italian style, it looks a little incongruous in this otherwise typical Cheshire country town. A second building, the Gaskell Memorial Tower, is also his work. It commemorates the author Elizabeth Gaskell, well-known for her novel 'Cranford' which was based on the town and people of Knutsford.

Left and below: Lyme Hall, near Disley. The Orangery with Minton tiled floor. The house is of Elizabethan origin with 18th and 19th century additions. (National Trust).

Lamaload reservoir, in the hills above Bollington
and Rainow.

Opposite: Little Moreton Hall, perhaps the best known half-timbered building anywhere in England. Construction began in 1480 and reached its final form about 100 years later. (National Trust).

Below: The courtyard of Little Moreton Hall.

Left: Langley Hall.*

Below: Langley reservoir.

Opposite page,
above: Macclesfield Forest.

Below: Langley reservoir in winter.

Below: Mow Cop. A mock castle built in 1754 as a summer house, set on a high rocky outcrop on the border with Staffordshire.

Opposite: Marton, near Congleton. The church of St. James and St. Paul is one of the oldest timber framed churches in Europe. It was founded and endowed by Sir John de Davenport in 1345.

The Manchester Ship Canal skirts the edge of the county, following the banks of the River Mersey until it heads inland from Widnes towards Manchester.

Right: Malpas. St. Oswald's church (14th century).

Below: The old Market House, built in 1762.

Left: Macclesfield. The 108 steps up to the parish church.

Below: Macclesfield Town Hall.

Manchester International Airport, near Styal.

Nether Alderley Mill. Dates from the 16th
century, with machinery of 1850 in full working
order. (National Trust).

This page and opposite: Nantwich. From Roman times until the end of the 18th century, this market town was the centre of the English salt industry. The town centre around the square still retains many of the black & white Elizabethan buildings and narrow winding streets.

Below: Churches Mansion.

Opposite: Norton Priory. The remains of an Augustinian priory established in 1134 and dissolved by Henry VIII in 1536.

Below: Lion Salt Works, Northwich. Northwich is one of the three Cheshire salt towns (with Nantwich and Middlewich) and the Lion Works was the only salt factory in the country still using the 'open pan' method, before its closure.

Left: The Town Bridge over the River Weaver at Northwich, an adjustable water-supported swing bridge.

Below: Northwich.

Orchard, near Cholmondeley.

OVERTON HALL FARM,
near Malpas. Makers of real
farmhouse Cheshire cheese.

Left: Overton Hall Farm.

Below: Some of the herd of 129 Friesian cows.

Right: After rennet is added to the milk, curds form and sink to make a solid block, which is chopped coarsely and the whey drained off.

Below left: Salt is added to the chopped curds, as a preservative and to enhance the flavour of the cheese.

Below right: Large pieces of curd are fed into a grinding mill to make small granules. These are then put into moulds to dry out. 60lbs of wet curd makes a 50lb cheese.

Over page: The finished cheese is completely covered in muslin and wax to keep it moist and fresh.

The Peckforton Hills, a sharp sandstone ridge
north-east of Malpas.

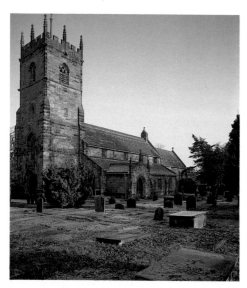

Left: Prestbury. St. Peter's church.

Below: The Norman chapel in the churchyard, Prestbury.

Rainow, set in the hills above Macclesfield.

ROLLS ROYCE

The most prestigious motor car in the world is made at Crewe. These pictures demonstrate some of the high levels of skill and craftsmanship which go into the production of these wonderful cars.

Overleaf
Top: Body shells being inspected before priming and painting.

Below: Engine assembly and checking.

Opposite

Top left: Engine blocks stacked outside to remove stresses in the metal.

Below left: Patterns laid out for cutting the pieces of English hide upholstery. Records and amounts of hide are kept so that exact repairs can be made.

Top right: The radiator grilles are entirely assembled by hand.

Below right: The burr walnut veneer used for the dashboard (and other) trim is hand cut and carefully matched for pattern and colour.

Opposite: A Rolls Royce Silver Spirit complete and ready for its owner.

Below: Risley Moss. The old peat cutting area on the raised bogland is now a nature reserve of open heathland and pools.

Opposite: The bridge from Runcorn to Widnes, across the River Mersey.

Right and below: Redesmere, near Capesthorne Hall.

Rostherne Mere, close to the M56 and the main Altrincham to Northwich road. It is a nature reserve which can be seen from the road into the village.

Rostherne village. Former estate workers cottages.

Opposite: Silk weaving at the Paradise Mill. The weaving of silk began in Macclesfield in the 1750s and this mill housed the last hand loom business in the town.

Above left: Jacquard handlooms.

Below left: Many fine strands of silk make up the pattern of warp threads.

Below: Shutlingsloe, one of the county's landmarks.

Below and opposite: Styal: Quarry Bank Mill. A fine Georgian cotton mill, now owned by the National Trust. Some of the looms have been restored to working order and make calico, which is printed and made up into garments for sale in many of the Trust's shops.

Stanlow oil refineries, near Ellesmere Port.

Below and opposite: All Saints, Siddington. Not what it seems–the lively black & white west end is actually painted onto brick. Underneath the brick is the original half-timbering, which had to be reinforced by the brick cladding in 1815, as the walls were bulging due to the weight of the heavy flag-stone roof.

Left: Saxon stone crosses in Sandbach market place.

Below: Stretton Mill, near Farndon.

Below: The Eagle and Child–the coat of arms of the Stanley family of Alderley Edge. The estate is now owned by ICI (Pharmaceuticals Division).

Opposite: The view across Macclesfield Forest from Tegg's Nose in summer and winter.

Left: Tatton Park. The Japanese garden.

Below: Tatton Hall, near Knutsford. Left to the National Trust in 1958 by Lord Egerton, with a collection of furniture, pictures and family memorabilia.

Upland Cheshire

Left: Wilmslow. Romany's Caravan. Romany was a naturalist and broadcaster whose radio nature trails were popular with children of all ages.

Below: White Nancy. On the tip of Kerridge Hill, this white bell-shaped structure is a landmark for miles around.

The old reflected in the new. Warrington.

Below and next page: The magnificent gates of
Warrington Town Hall.

The hill village of Wincle.

Wildboarclough: The tiny parish church of
St. Saviour, built in 1908.

Below: Widnes. Spike Island–site of the birthplace of mass chemical production. The Yorkstone slab was the base of one of the Gossage Towers at Hutchinson no. 1 works, which condensed hydrogen chloride by the Leblanc process. The towers were about 60ft high and built of Yorkstone, filled with bricks.

Opposite: Sunset on the Dee estuary, from the Wirral peninsula looking across to North Wales.